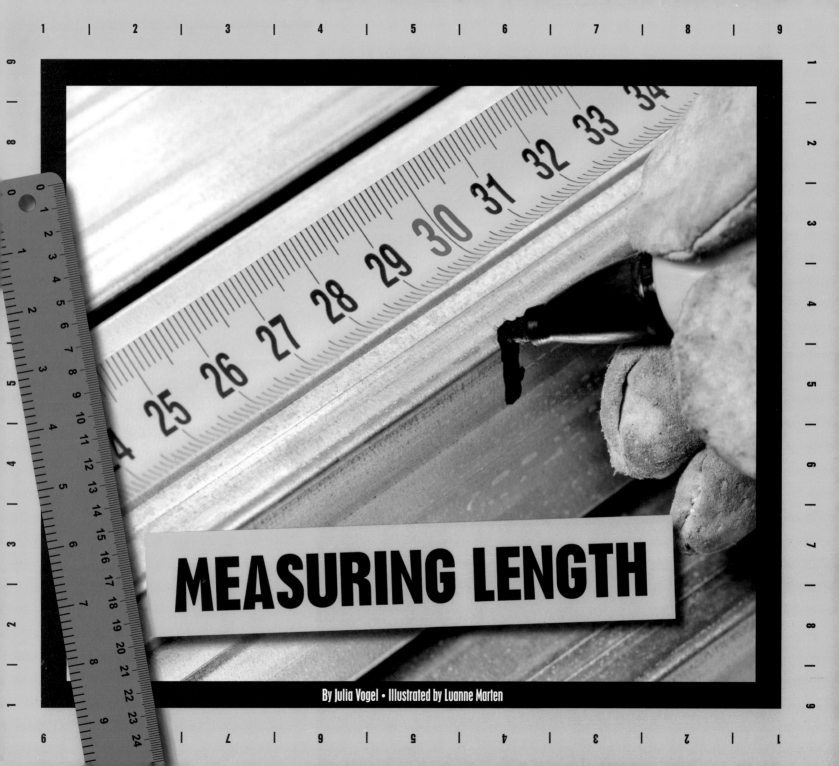

MEASURING LENGTH

By Julia Vogel • Illustrated by Luanne Marten

The Child's World®

Published by The Child's World®
1980 Lookout Drive • Mankato, MN 56003-1705
800-599-READ • www.childsworld.com

Acknowledgments
The Child's World®: Mary Berendes, Publishing Director
The Design Lab: Cover and interior design
Amnet: Cover and interior production
Red Line Editorial: Editorial direction

Photo credits
Dmitry Naumov/iStockphoto, cover, 1; Shutterstock Images, cover, 1, 2; Monkey Business
Images/Shutterstock Images, 5; Eric Isselée/Shutterstock Images, 11; Zebrin Yakov/
Shutterstock Images, 12; Eric Broder Van Dyke/Shutterstock Images, 15; Sonya Etchison/
Shutterstock Images, 19; Monique Rodriguez/iStockphoto, 23

ISBN 9781614732792
LCCN 2012933661

Printed in the United States of America
Mankato, MN
July 2012
PA02121

ABOUT THE AUTHOR

Award-winning author Julia Vogel has a bachelor's degree in biology and a doctorate in forestry. Julia has four kids (Eli is the shortest) and three cats (Miss Lemon is the widest).

ABOUT THE ILLUSTRATOR

Luanne Marten has been drawing for a long time. She earned a bachelor's degree in art and design from the University of Kansas. She has four grown sons and one granddaughter who now has the shortest feet in the family.

TABLE OF CONTENTS

Lengthy Questions

Do you like to ask questions?
　　Who is taller? Who has longer feet?
Who has the shortest pet?
　　How can you find the answers?
By measuring length!

You can measure your family's feet to see how long they are.

Are your feet longer than your friends' feet?

AN ARM'S LENGTH
Long ago, Egyptians measured with units called cubits. This is the distance from the elbow to the tip of the middle finger of a grown man.

Real Feet for Feet

Before people had **standard** tools for measuring, they used body parts. They might use a hand, an arm, or a foot.

How long is your foot? Trace it on a piece of paper. Then cut out the tracing. Compare your tracing to a friend's.

Now stand next to a wall. Ask your friend to measure your height with the tracing of your foot. How many "feet" tall are you? Then measure your height with your friend's foot tracing. Did you get different answers with different tracings?

Feet and other body parts come in different sizes. People saw they needed one standard unit. In Rome, a grown man's foot was chosen as the standard. A stick one "foot" long became the unit of measure.

A man's foot length became the standard measurement.

Smaller Parts

A ruler is a good tool for measuring your height. But what if you're measuring something small, like a tiny dog? Then you need a smaller measuring unit.

Romans divided the foot into 12 equal parts called inches. With a ruler marked in inches, you can tell which pup is shorter—and by how much.

Let's say your dog is 25 inches tall. A friend's dog is 10 inches tall. Your dog is 15 inches taller than your friend's pup! (25 inches minus 10 inches is 15 inches.)

You can use a ruler to measure the height of cats and dogs.

centimeters

inches

Some rulers have both inches and centimeters on them.

Feet or Meters?

People in the United States use the **US customary system**. This means they use feet and inches to measure.

But most of the world uses the **metric system**. In this system, the basic unit is the meter. One meter is a little more than 3 feet long. A meter can be divided evenly into 10 decimeters or 100 centimeters.

Miles to Go

Sometimes you need to measure long distances, such as a football field. You can use yards instead of feet. One yard equals 3 feet in length. A football player who runs from goal to goal runs 100 yards, or 91.4 meters.

What about something even longer? Would you say it is 5,280 feet to the park? No way! For really long distances you can use miles. One mile is 5,280 feet. In the metric system, kilometers are used. One mile is just over 1.6 kilometers.

A football field is measured in yards. White lines cross the field to mark 10 yards.

Measure round things with a string.

AROUND AND AROUND
How big around is your backpack? Wrap a string around it. Then measure the string for the answer!

Not So Straight

Not everything you measure is a straight line. How do you measure things that are crooked?

Something curvy can be measured with a string. Then hold the string up to a ruler. You can also use a measuring tape that bends easily. A measuring tape is useful for round things, such as a tree trunk. A giant redwood may measure more than 90 feet (27.4 meters) around!

Guesswork

What if you don't have a measuring tool? You can **estimate**, or make a good guess. To guess a short length, try using a fingertip for a half-inch. Licorice that is 10 fingertips long is about 5 inches of a tasty treat.

To guess a far distance, count your steps. Romans said 1,000 steps by a grown man is 1 mile. But for you it'll be a little more. Count your steps from your home to your best friend's. How far away is her home?

Next, use a tool to check your estimates. Were you a good guesser? Or did you miss by a mile?

Count your steps to a friend's house to estimate how far away it is.

US Customary and Metric

1 inch = 2.5 centimeters
1 foot = .3 meter
1 yard = .9 meter
1 mile = 1.6 kilometers

1 centimeter = .4 inch
1 meter = 3.3 feet or 1.1 yards
1 kilometer = .6 mile

Try to remember these US customary and metric units.

Measure It Out

Confused by all the different units? Here's a table to help you keep them straight.

12 inches = 1 foot
3 feet = 1 yard
5,280 feet = 1 mile

100 centimeters = 1 meter
1000 meters = 1 kilometer

Measuring Mania

Now you can answer questions by measuring. You can tell in inches or centimeters who is taller, whose feet are longer, and who has the shortest pet.

What other questions can you answer? Grab your ruler and start measuring!

DO THE MATH
Make sure you keep track of units when doing measurement math. You can only add numbers that have the same units. Inches go with inches. Meters go with meters, and so on!

A girl measures how far she jumped in a track-and-field event.

Glossary

estimate (ES-tuh-mate): To estimate means to make an educated guess to find out the value, amount, or distance of something. You can estimate distance by counting your steps.

metric system (MEH-trik SIS-tuhm): The metric system is a system of measuring based on the meter. The metric system is used around the world.

standard (STAN-durd): A standard is an idea or thing used to measure or compare other things. A foot became a standard for measuring length.

units (YOU-nits): Units are standard amounts used to measure. Inches and centimeters are units for length.

US customary system (YOO-es KUS-tuh-mer-ee SIS-tuhm): The US customary system is a system of measuring that uses feet, inches, and miles. The United States uses the US customary system.

Books

Cleary, Brian P. *How Long or How Wide? A Measuring Guide.* Minneapolis, MN: Millbrook Press, 2007.

Maxwell, Yolanda. *Famous Bridges of the World: Measuring Length, Weight, and Volume.* New York: Rosen Publishing, 2005.

Web Sites

Visit our Web site for links about measuring length: **childsworld.com/links**

Note to Parents, Teachers, and Librarians: We routinely verify our Web links to make sure they are safe and active sites. So encourage your readers to check them out!

Index